SOMETHING

FOR

EVERYBODY

SOMETHING

ANSELM BERRIGAN

WAVE BOOKS SEATTLE AND NEW YORK

FOR

EVERYBODY

Published by Wave Books

www.wavepoetry.com

Wave Books titles are distributed to the trade by

Consortium Book Sales and Distribution

Phone: 800-283-3572 / SAN 631-760X

Library of Congress Cataloging-in-Publication Data

Designed and composed by Quemadura

Printed in the United States of America

9 8 7 6 5 4 3 2 1

First Edition

Wave Books 074

What?

Nothing

SOMETHING

FOR

EVERYBODY

WHAT THE STREETS LOOK LIKE

Mom: the sweet rotted
summer stench still
taps the nasal cavity
inside breezes several
times per block. I have
a greater empathy for
pigeons after two months
at work in the unnatural
country, & find it
instinctively nerve-
wracking to remove my
wallet from its pocket
here in town despite
the general lack of threat.
The streets look grey
nonplussed, post-
pubescent relative to
ancient times but
nonetheless grid-wizened
in the face of an ever-
changing lineup of
banks, bars, and specialty
shops with their weak
signs and distant tones
(lighting). Second Ave
is giving up, slowly

its cheap depth store-
front by storefront.
One feels less than
nostalgic for the like-
lihood of being mugged
but likelihood itself
feels less than evident
unless one is being
unstable and unspoken
coming to dreaming
while pushing a stroller
over the variously cracked
slabs of concrete each
block yet greets the
wheels with. The right
part of the y heading
west on tenth between
2nd and 3rd is still
tree-lined and aristocratic
as feint, though its
sidewalk looks like
late Auden's smoked
cheeks. I loathe it,
amiably, when Sylvie
is asleep.

TO A COPY

It was less

          than exciting

                    being itself

less than excitable
seeing you be
yourself

as emblem
of ideas with
a capital I, you

                           nowhere in sight, ceaselessly
                  referred to as missing, I totally got it

got the getting

the inert form generally fucked
the pockets of edification disclaiming reality
or some tenebrous, fibrous, bulbous, and bat-shit tumescent

demi-othering you care to fold into our vanguardianed creases. You pre-
ferred to print the note that came with. This other you came across as an emaciated assassin of

tranquility, wallowing
in a mudless parody of eternity's mist
for the dolly dolly grill

I feel bound to you
but I can't love you
can't work up the
intermittence, the

uncontrollable banal
discontinuity necessary
to love and by extension blend into your carefully handled telegraph of marginal
perceptivity.

Nothing
gets to be real
or realized
    or reality-based
        or filmed as if happening
            or rendered realistically
                or branded contemporary
                    or performed spontaneously
                        or reverse-engineered inappropriately
                            or propped up to appear live
                                or accused of being in the moment when I'm with you

and while I re-cognize my sins
                    I re-fuse to defeat them
            because I truly can see them
and by all we mutually hold dear
                    I do not believe in them

TILEBREAKER

I was busy
with frivolity
& its pursuit
of intellect
when this dig
poked head
from screen
and said, dude
bring fist down
to table & I thought
well, what does
make me happy
other than the
absolute mystery
of composition
with specific regard
to feeling thing's
inscrutable range
of depth
immediacy
& creeping
action on the ever
unready to be
pleasant mind?
The first thirty-six
seconds of Polvo's

Tilebreaker
for one, & as
it turns out
you can read
The New Spirit
and listen to
On The Mouth
on headphones
on the L train
beginning with
a G, & there's
something tran-
sistent about
the two at once
the looked at
listening of sitting
and reading while
the singer sings
"clean is not a
state that's real"
& maybe that
would be in
The New Spirit
or not, but pull-
ulating does drop
by, & the post-
punk position
as complanation
of "I'm ready to
leave again" drops
by repeatedly to
begin and begin
and begin, & it's

less clear to me
now as to how
war and aesthetics
sit in temporal
relation to one
another as both
are and are not
ignored, and endless
war doesn't quite
greet endless aesthetics
or perhaps they
touch like two
digitally composed
globes that animate
one globular unreal
& easily perceived
something on the
verge of something
else so one may be
the old moved mover
of yore, though
interconnection is
a military invention
isn't it, and art is
always usually x
amount of years
behind military tech
and ditching beauty
hasn't exactly shortened
the gap, but ditching
irritation is no help
either. I keep wanting
to dig The Hurting

which must have
worked very hard
for me in an older
continuous present
but I only get a few
good seconds from
each tune, though
the Banshees and
Kiss Them For Me
almost shockingly
gives minutes, & 3
Feet High And Rising
joyfully conjures
embarrassment—
I literally needed
a piece of rug to cut
slide, move the feet
without lift this
one Buffalo eve
in the deep of an
antigathering comp-
lex of quadrangle
living: all those
permutations
in sample form
of rock and soul
so oddly delicate
as to feel unvanished
in time without
resembling memory.

FOR GREGORY MICHAELIDIS

THE PARLIAMENT OF REALITY

Padre camouflage renders the top ambiguous
which is awesome, but it's hard to dial in on
the awesomeness of that extra layer of enclosure

May I have a sip of your cigarette, asleep
in all my clothes, crying, uselessly, as your singularity
apologizes for & preserves our long way around
to an open muted slightly flittering love?

Loitering is a primary talent reflamed
as needed between coming tensions: I don't want
the references, I want to be irritated, & freaked out
uneven in the fur, away from live wave domains, pushed
up hard against this or that delicately figured
boulder, a sprained delicacy absorbing biogenetic
prepositions masked as populated frequency
the illusion of daily non-acknowledgment

        Insomniac as a fool failing to order
a proper structure of bloodletting. See those birds
measuring any available appearances? They're poised
to join local gyms &, space begetting such mild
dissolution, universalize their bitching wings.

the green lake is awake

the green clock is a lock

the green flake is a lake

the green top is a shop

the lime green mop is a flop

the lime green pop is a lock

the lime green lime is a chime

the sea green rhyme climbed into the chimney

the chimney collapsed into aquamarine

the light green is bright green

the ever green is never seen

WITH SYLVIE BERRIGAN & COSIMA HILL

SPEECH

SMASH THEM.

EAT THEM.

SEVEN

When I was seven
in 1979, I'd go buy
the paper, for my
father, from Oscar's
dark green newsstand
on the corner of first
avenue & St. Mark's
Place. Oscar always
called me Oscar when
I stopped by. "Thanks
Oscar," he'd say as
I handed him the
quarter. "Bye Oscar"
I'd say, turning
around, going
back on my way.

SELF-PORTRAIT WITH LASERS

my fellow parenthetical palliative rodeos   inward beavises

tender chicken tenders   bullshit is a star

uncanny midlife anytime glub   speaking necrotics

not bad for a prototype   my loadedings hurt

scumbag fame   for missionary   milk thistling

postlinoleum palavers   trumping helioscopic deep depth

to terrorize drones   with ugly gentle cadavers   freelings

cultlines   missectioned living   actualization of ghosts

topiary pratfallen minaret-més   swaddle all lozenges   bounce their bobs

a t for twitchy eros   she ain't gonna give me five   & here comes horseshoe downturn

pre-sob   sobs   weaponized emphasis

indulging limits like taste   at least our bones aren't wet   right, daddy?

FOR MICHAEL GIZZI

proloblems

PRECISION AUTO

These prefab greens are part of a sale system
of red dots reserved for those whose demise

we thought predetermined by the timing
of their abuses. You sleep under a stitched

face sold for warmth between scales. Extreme
snowfall, memorial readings of butterfly attacks

on Seventh Ave, and the exile's octuplets
refuse Dream's capacity to give waking outline

of body to I who were alive. The restroom
is for steel cut customers wearing expensive

jackets three sizes too small. There's something
insidious about this music one pays to listen

for, the perk of employment lacerating
the ears of our artifice to form a profile of

togetherness. That rap jaked an emerald
game to con every concept of elsewhere

Dilated pupils following local smoke signals
trading that rainbow beaten down to tears

for a greasier grill from which to pay the bills
Pre-judgment's an overly natural affect anyhow

dusky matter in need of cosmic perversion
We see your indifference, and raise you

an impractical salute. There's no bond
of reality between money and enough

POEM FOR LOS ANGELES

Pigeons fly to the birthday

But for the ones on the ground

Taking a walk on the rocks

Thinking about chasing another

Pigeon going around the garbage

Thinking about flags in the sky

Moving and thinking about being flags

And eating the pigeons all up!

The big statue of the lion over there

Is mad at the people and thinking

About RAH!! (interlude to chase

Pigeons) Come back! Stroller sees

A big frog and the stroller cries

Want to say goodbye to anybody?

Yes. Who? You. See you later. I'm

Going to chase all those pigeons

WITH SYLVIE BERRIGAN

POEM FOR CIRCULATION

Things surrounding things
fill my Wicked Tuna grid

heart with a swishy austerity-like
intention. I cut my post-fleshy

forearms & bleed a serious parallel
echo chamber reading everything

to approve of nothing. I massage
my anterior cruciate ligaments

to celebrate a hard-won royal flush.
This mind is slick-like and easy-like

and music-like and gesture-like
and, as I am the dappled heathen

you've been given internal permission
to dismiss from your sacrosanct

barricades and bounty systems,
coy, and shit-like. A second first-person

recapitulation does not defiantly
buy shape rightly here. Sane

continuity is *your* trashy blues
making progress out of heart's lack.

How should *I* know you're not
there bleeding, respectably

to conclude a moist relentment
and make my evil labors clear?

POEM

Mocking model on table helps

Hate my exploding (again) pen

She insists upon ignoring from

Her cover the iffy chromatics

Of the Curie hospital's petit

Waiting room, little squares

Of color posting up hyper-bored

On passing surfaces, they surface

To pass me, I like to tell myself

Waiting for Mom to finish up

Some surgery, why the locked

Closet given one narrow door

Of dour burgundy & one drab

Pink companion of Hardyish

Width? A standoff of chairs ignores

The question, I'm a know-nothing

Volunteer, unable to receive the

Latest round of passwords: type

Havok101 to access Curie wifi

Ohwystan to retract claws, winspear-

Ranch to retrieve half chicken in

Future dressing from timewich

Likes resisting clouds by naming

The fantasy of café life its own

Stumbling paperwork a floating head

Thing thinks on way out to exercise

A fear of ordering, "it" now as always

A demonstration against competence

NEW NOTE

weekend voids quickly fill the throng, the song's importance retelling what you've witnessed under-sea, out windows at declines, stranger proposes to sandwich, the little boxes filled with deregulated words making snuff films for sound, they follow me into pants, one-quarter recognize anyone wash-ing a kid-sized head, em-dashes fall out the munchkin's ear

but if I'm gonna fake the sag, get bad at invitation, disexamine little planar warts between fingers, lead the evening around by its dissident ass, convert all critical meetings into hot tubs, the wallpaper makes a break for enthusiasm, no, I'm just enthusiastically useless or hated by little e, leopard print eyelids get that plasma welding machine out mouth please

Edwin levitating the church said soda scoured his perimeter to give her space untied little ribbons the gum pavements compositions let rise, the phone thinks it needs to send out its chapters, but my weepilies keep being dissolves into lists, would someone please hand me that Morandi? I stole a wee de Kooning from the pinocchio museum in D from Ohio

put it under my jackathon and elopitated with peoples made a mistake with me early on, it's ok though, it's part of them and me, photo of bloody sky undresses on desktop, everyone who dies before I'm born keeps being influenced by me and the half-hole, crib performance zone, a mock school receding into outlines Stuyvesant Fish makes

a pitch for plaque life, flesh dunce, fingered by fog, the kitty implies waving forever, phony greet-ings forever, or should we say real greetings with phony tonalities the crackademies dub affect after fact, O Pierre! we should have come over for the midnight omelette, but do you know hard it is to be alive & not steal the state mace with a mutating bag

of tricks touching flights with the touched? the suns are falling fast, adjunct suns at one-fifth warmth writhe into contributor copies, at the end of the mouth, endure they longer the selves around sen-sation accumulate images without eye sockets, everything gets done, it was always an anti-cop it around here, and and as slowly growing rolled

MUST IMPROVE

A.

Elegance factor.
Distention.
Kindness to strangers.
Imagination.
Contours of appearance.
Ability to give off.
Plural you.
Escape hatch.
Congressional Meal of Honor.
Sanity bar.
Savory goods.
Affair with resemblance.
Condition of pants.
Distortion.
Vehicle management.
Dream memory.
Anything.

B.

An oblique measure
of health; correspondence
to (with?) objects
categorized in nature;

spontaneity less chance;
chance less order; shape
& consistency of secrets;
timing; ability to withhold
statements designed to
provoke reinforcement
I neither trust nor need;
unironical use of "dig";
ability, once solid, to
vibrate wordlessly in good
company; recognition;
attention; disconnection
from access to ideas.

VEINS & MODES & VEINS & MODES & VEINS & MODES & VEINS & MODES & VEINS & MODES &

Scratched to like in a fall clanging
The on to on for hope, an again

        Erupts we finders, specklife most
        Likely an 11-seed. Specklife is a

Flotative gardening puking at every
Front. Specklife is boneless or

            Traditional, stealing bowling balls
            Alien lanes long to miss. One plus

        One is nothing if noticeable, a
        Conjugated in-law, a pillar of the

                Humanskyite interviewable boof
                A spatial inversion, absorbing hurled

            Replicant doll ships. Ads know what
            One plus one means. But cameras &

                Their pet eyeballs, the orientation
                Of horizon lines, do not set us at

        Ease, dodging folding volumes. One
        Plus one is looking at a cornfield

From an intergalactic perspective
& walking through it at the same

Time, semi-fucked as that half-
Sounds in the late March sleetlight

One plus one greets for company
We like a bilanguid hinge about now

FOR ED STECK

17 MINI-ESSAYS ON *THE COLLECTED WRITINGS OF JOE BRAINARD*

PROBLEMS

And then at the very moment of appreciation I had no problem.

THE FRIENDLY WAY

"Our swordfish just had eleven babies and I'm not at all sure what to do with them."

NANCY

Nancy was always handing me jars that I couldn't open.

READING

Strange to read her because I can only do so by somehow pretending to *be* her.

COVER-UP

I think that a lot of people think "being a nice person" is just a cover-up. I don't think so. Or, if it is, it's a better cover-up than most.

ON THE BUS

I'm never totally convinced, riding a bus, that I'm on the right bus.

HOPE

I hope people know I don't *want* to glance away, or down, sometimes, when we are talking.

TURNS

My work never turns out like I think it is going to. I start something. It turns into a big mess. And then I clear up the mess.

HAVING A SHOW

If you want to know what it's like to have the rug pulled out from under you (don't bother) (and besides, I'm sure you already know) try having a show.

MUSEUM OF NATURAL HISTORY

This would be an interesting place to "trip".

THAT FEELING

What defines that feeling one has when staring at a rock?

TWO HAIRS PAST A FRECKLE

I remember "Two hairs past a freckle" when someone asks you what time it is and you don't have a watch.

HARD HURT

(Hard hurt.)

TAKING CREDIT

That honest is only something you can *try* to be. (If you want to be.) And I do. But I don't want to have to take credit for *being* honest.

MATCHES

It seems I am always looking for matches.

DREAMS

Dreams to me are a sort of bonus.

A BEAUTIFUL BUTT

There is nothing I find more beautiful than a really beautiful butt.

LOADING

That pen don't have any good
Poems in it. It's tired of this old

World & its colorless fiascos
& ungodly extensions for obvious

Performance Enhancing Drug
Users. Implied hyphenated

Linebacker hinge for projection:
We's all think it's bad but disagree

On what the definition of it is.
Expect to be killed by otherwise

Docile poets when they get inside
The etcetera zone. Pronk adds a win

In the abstract. Your and my
Naturalized self, which we've let

Interview ye but refuse to let be
Ye is being followed by drones

Built by big bugs in old walls.
As it was time to get serious I

Split. Don't need no astrology.
Anyway you're down on the

Street, disclaiming the I feel
Radish of the digitally impaired.

You're a cold-spleened brofuck-
Er, I guess. How come people are

Only mostly prone in description?
I don't think about kinds of things.

All Pirate hamstrings retire as
Pirates extend Hurdle. Scary fake

Talker over there scares me
Briefly, but still, I can't wait

To screed Dredd Judd amidst
The untalkers I solitaire usselves

With. A vaguely confident human
Just told us Wall St's closed

Today, so why we looking so
Involved? I thought I wanted

To be serious right nowness:
My body told me to be serious:

But I don't know: "Did your
Daddy have video games when

You were a girl?" the little girl
Asks. She's so damn large I

Almost can't correct us. About
Now I hear John Yau asking

For a word. Leopards confronted
With mirrors dig the woods

According to nihilist cheeseballs
With fancy frames. We get

Knocked down at recess too
Sweety. Hi Bears! If you see

A graffitied skull on the phone
That's a temporary we: A is

for Atalantavan. B is for Broke-
Ass Daddy. Z is for moustache.

I is for I Don't Get It, home in
time for the horrors of selection.

LOADEDING

A filmer films for footage of
Singers singing to strangers

Begging off encouragement but
Me no like that song: drag brain

Into timeout. *Fuck*. Wrong train
The doc was being shot on a six

I split for the Q, too stupid
To not see an R. You & your

Signals & codes: I feel like a
Condescendant's objectivity

Watching from the rim
Of a spicy bucket. Accezzible

Liar. On 1,150 buses citizenries
Get to feel the experience of simple

Complexity, complex complexity
& complex simplicity; & simple

Simplicity. & surveillance cameras
To make you smile. O giraffes O

Hippo videos O plotzed under-
Ground O unknown knowns

Abandoned by charismatic save-
Us-from-fear desk-dick defense

Calculations O piles of bodies
Taking it everywhere & here

LIFE WITHOUT RONDO

Recordings made when no
one's there, that's what we like.

Too many scraps full of pockets.
We agree, but clause. Always.

A punk rock lunch on sidewalk,
stakesters plummeting from

condimental tips. I'm implying
for jobs by writing you, despite

your sounding Beatles-chafed
echoes of phone aroma carolina

gold. We like it when I writes, not
when we make type. Wondering

where John calls home for brief
bio scrubs on the, the web. "In a bow,

dad." Right. I knew that cadence
picked me up somewhere. It, like

McDonald's, is coming off. Service
interruptions, we like those triple

bonus mattress sales a lot. Bonus
is a filthy excuse for a word, words.

That's why we torched Jared. It's not
enough to know what things mean

beaten off to the side, fool. Sometimes
you gotta know what things don't mean.

LENGTHENING ARCHES

I gave up early on the search
for the source, taking halting
steps along my recovery, yet
it was not so wracked with
difficulty, that disavowal of
energies one conjures from
pictures of plagues. I had some
images, their fleeting contours
bred to provoke a system of
scanning I'd later teach others
to acknowledge and lose. That's
taking credit for waking up again
and we don't like that. Three
encourages bad decisions, hand-
drawn to simulate the time
stolen at the well-lit end of the
street. But I desist from remarking
upon your infallibility with
relation to proper naming of the
local avian. Someone picked
up a hawk's name, I forgot it
told someone else it had a name
though clearly not taking part
in the act, the hawk I mean
with regards to nonparticipation
a certain protest on my part

this forgetting, and daily I
resist looking its name up on
the web, to keep things unreal.
And that's the shit I get for
attempting to separate nature
from naming, another set of
giggling decisions taunting us
as we delve into the drop off
service. That said, you may
certainly borrow the seat next
to me, elevated as it might
be, if homogeneous with
shadowy distinction. But
I take pleasure in the fact
that our opinions often have
the honor of coinciding
with yours, and that we follow
them, though far behind
proclaiming their ruddy virtues.
We're surrounded by testimony
to the will of organic processes
as they depart from their means
and breed plastic flocks of time-
resistant doves. On page four
the king of the sea and his
battle penguins ward off their
colorful enemies, or so a scan
re-reveals on a hunt for spoilers
in the deep night. I can't wait
for you to operate. I apologize
for using the word procedure.
I kicked the chair nearby, right
in its red, and said "sorry

chair." 'Tis not so necessary
as it once was to fear and
consider the present tense
and plight of the cannibal,
but I can't help think these
times infected by a deeper
meanness than savagery. Though
yeah, illusions are a dime a
dozen and the twenty, that
yuppie food stamp, will net
you many minutes' worth of
illusory surfaces if you're a
savvy shopper: these liquid
antioxidants for instance;
that book of wisdom a half
millennium old; the red velvet
cupcakes tempting us from
behind the counter. The signs
for the washing of hands instill
a thickening resentment toward
dirt's absence as we navigate
the gaps between moments of
silence. These upside-down
blank white pages reek of
humility, which is what seaward
tenement but a mid-air
cluster bomb teasing your
material comforts under its
so-called protection. Wassup
guys? How you doing? This
is Wanda. She wiped out the
mutant population with an
utterance then vanished until

redrawn this very evening.
Spirituality, human emotion
the weight loss of history, and
selved identity: these would
be little remarkable in such a
scheme if they didn't produce
caducous cacophony. But it's
sad, I like to touch the parts
to be the last person to touch
the part that's coming off.

JUNE AT ONE ON AVE A

Bus!

Bus!

O bus. . . . .

JIM BRODEY

It's getting hard to have me around too Jim
So I write you under yellow light leaning
Into some waylaid framed dimensions tearing off

Them from reapers may Joan Mitchell's oils leap
Off their canvases & drown the neo-fangled supremacist
Cops advancing on the water protectors at DAPL

The heart of the breath wakes up on a screeching
Bench in the park-skein veins' excavated twirl
Of holes do holes twirl Jim do you speak to

Sullen children in the after-breath of hoisted wooden
Woo bouncing off trained belches into tantrums of
Refusal until some sugary bribe arrives triggering

Departure I have three & a half jobs which is
Three too many when I said get me in for free
To the sky addressing you addressing it I imagined

A band composed from your trashbag of tapes
Lines harder to carry slipping under the nails
Tom R. checked out recently to twenty versions in

Twenty languages of Tottering State going at once
The construction workers buzzing outside's intimation
Of locust abortion technician agree the cackling

Was beautiful if overly kempt for subroutine
Bum phasers on slow withdrawal from the
Whomp-clod headlight eternities of slush

Hour traffic you go that way & scout out the
Other direction you wake up & actually speak
You amplify Breathlehem into collector's edition

I never tell what I take from it's taken every
Try to get the shape of a thing even a little
Bright flowers painted from their lifelike listen

JIM BRODEY

You're just going to find yourself yelling at clouds
If you wake up & dive into info-bits first thing
Last thing & what cloud wouldn't whistle back

If you cooed its way straight up neck craned ob-
Structing the arrhythmatic piecemealdom of street
Traffic by serenading cirruses with your right to be

Judged by your best bent tonal escapades you &
The pigeons rising up and defecating down to wish
Good luck upon the sucker denizens of our on-

Going charade of linear experience to intrude
For intoxicate silly promises so reflect as agleam
Night with wander portraits heat reveal fucking

Merging the Hesiod Dylan tapes hippityhopping
Straight regal unplugged warm an old chaos
Begrets heads of mild comport for loving in purses

We all need heads to carry around in purses to
Protect from the nonpigeon life forms swirling
Around our daily ant wars & primal odes to

Carelessness one convention hides another locker
Portal to convention's gigantor half-life a jar
Of conserved tears in the wallpaper fabric of

Reality dead in a song for a pepsi a karnak in a
Green hoodie with teleporting dog dammit Jim
All the leaves live in flown-under facetime

Fantasies of sanity you'd have to structure some
Bullpen usage around champagne Jujyfruits
Marvelous as Aquaman on a melodious

Afternoon come over & sit down forever tell
Me all the ways in silence we don't exploit
Our traumas together I'm a feather not a leak

JIM BRODEY

Here is a contradiction involving time
Here's a counterfrictional hairy seat
Devolving time & time's uncle shame

Here's a bobbleheaded Jehovah spotless
And wicked as a wide-orbited unemotional
Lamb cutting off its gibby-tripped legs

To dance one-legged in the rain in
Florida Here is an I am defrosted defronted
Decrusted decustardized & dedappled

Yours with dwarf star lips anything surrounds
Claude Monet was one of these heiresses a
Flying horse of wild crab language more

Face under Here's vicious deportation squalor
Here is a counterfactual spotlight for loveless
Professionals all desire they meet as illusion

Here let me a a if let there glow on and we
Here is so only stars writhing out street free
Herein and grace there this or violent will dealings

Hear that firing marvelous on when she bespeaks
Hearish rampant moronic palatial mind to Mr
Here buckles a pioneer one reacheth whereas

Heres of him run explanation into when the this
Reveals likewise gone to vapor Here's a likewise
Pumping straight to your heart with a spliff of

Unsane word shape blastments shed rhythm's
Tortoise histories Here's guppy marginal talker's
A bent other cruising items all reborn armor

Reaching envelops where-separated tariff brains
Get-gots brained & rebrained by interior post-
Astral domain Here be trance Here be lanced

JIM BRODEY

I only hold against you your name and your pain
But for also holding up against you an Aussie
Python stuck between engine and oven mitt

No I truly hold against you your belief your
Name is yours, is yours, is yours, the torture
Of disagreement, it's nearly become torture to

Disagree, where's that one star framed solely
For thee, Jim, you aren't the you here, I
Hold against myself the flimsy inability

To let myself go, completely, but only I
Hold that really can you believe it's a quarter
Century since you turned that last corner forever

& fake fucking news is all the rage? sorry
Not fake fucking just fake news—fake fuck-
Ing is as establishment as the national debt

Pop-song formula, single-issue plotz & shitty
Movies making suckers cry in surround sound
I will begin a campaign to claim my fake name

We're just shitting ideas these days Jim every
Other mug online's a Robert Moses building
Grass-free playgrounds in the mind rinds, oh

This negativity has to stop shopping itself
Around I only only hold cruelty against the vast
Nonbody grinding bodies into numbers &

I'm seriously worried about the gentle zen
Gem of Mundo, whose anger runs whispering
Away from him looking for a kindly host

Like me to play unto wraith didn't Eddie
Cook you broccoli once? All little kids secretly
Know how to cook for blues-addled bums

JIM BRODEY

All this shattering incredulous dull-minded
Speed all this slow burn ache Stockholm
Syndromed into cuckoo clusters of badass

Fucked upholstery all these endless Wystan
The cat w/superpowers stories for unsleeping
Munchkins demanding adult brooding go into

The wood chipper the cat could swing on
People swings go all the way around the sky
Bar travel by balloons inside balloons & stride

Across Saturn's rings just to check the grain of
Footing I should say pouring all the unbridled—
You been bridled lately?—love addressed to names

And me slumming at the sky church to get some
Something sums to come off the teen-death-shock
Chest were bald scalps or super-old-skinned beings

Scarier don't clean your floor ever I am a princess
Of bubbly nothingness & mean nothing all the lines
I steal from Jim to make this there slanky-ass poem

Who invented ass as a demi-adjectival modifier
Anyway—someone who knew the power of the
Ass-syllable in fits of rhetoric dawn & corner-yap

It's a precision-stress an undeniable slap of emphasis
That defeats its own generic-ass nonquality what
The fuck was we saying all the neoclassical mosaic

Brodey schmear I'm laying down to help me get
Through via unfashionable noncurrency this
Absolute disaster of a current state may there be

More hoary hosts of landings on this dark star as we
Dig to un-survive through and for the "one poem
We all write out of our entire existence alive"

INWARD BRANDING MECHANISM 2:
LONESOME SABOTAGE

Goodness is better than evil
Becuz it is nicer. I detest your

        Holding me so high in the air
        While I cry fat tears pre-bath

                Tap for more tweets, munch
                In the preserved meatlight

        Ballads without preservations
        Tidy outcome emblems

Hitching baggage to be verbs
Cartoon butchery, vulgar

        Phrasings, crosswalk-like
        Pauses, so we don't get hit

                No that's all duration disease
                Bespitting florigins. I can see

        Lateness blueing the ave B light
        In advance of what gets called

Spring. Go talk about some
Paintings you can't figure out

Shouldn't have thought about
You. Thought you were individual

Game tickets on sale. Moatful
Pre-listserv, hesitant in light of

The pickoff portents & mean
Like me. A simile for meanness

On the gravy train till doomsday
A monument to perseverance

INWARD BRANDING MECHANISM

Orderly rides. Don't give a speech
Change, for the rules of the way

Any sucker gets to be an opener
Of I can't stand the way. Subway's

Your seated brother. In your mind
Everything's harder & harder, and

You're the World Be Free of persons
Who write project economics! Don't

Know you by intelligentsia's design.
Next Stop: Playoffs sponsored by

"My apple pie kicks ass," looking
For Melmoth, or a quarter

Slightly feral (fetal) uncanny, more
Than 300 million pieces sold globally

Hot on The Heels of Slug Bait &
Other engineering mazes. Anselm

Is a niche poetess behind a window
Named nurture, doing the voice, saying

How at every pre-environment outset:
Donkey donkey donkey donkey donkey

FOR ANNE BOYER

INQUIRE WITHOUT

the men walked on in silence
passing by long ruins of stables
they walked through several
corridors in silence, passing
by several agen, the rest keeping
silence, passing by Roxanes, a
commander of a thousand men
trudging the rest of the way in
silence, passing by the Ichiraku
ramen stand and the library
drove east in silence, passing
by Hochstadt, Mönchenholzhausen
and Weimar, across new halls
of silence, passing by an old
and gigantic tree, which has
miraculous properties in the
hearts of those who are thus
in speechless and pensive silence
passing by the slamming stops
for a moment, the eerie silence
passing by again, until there is
one final large slam and the door
to rooms shatters open towards
Silence Passing by Paul Klee
strange moods of silence passing
by without word or comment
facts of striking interest & sig-
nificance, streams of awkward
people, & the silence at hand

ILLANELLE

A ginger ancestor played human by takes

Her tickling shines this discarded grinning

My jumbo warp fetish threadbare on the make

Got to get some tussy-mussy hefty flub mulched shake

Our think edge wears your me native brooding

Ankh ging-ginged ancestry humanish by stakes

My primary mode of contention's a glimpse. Flakes

Distress these weaselly saints. Their handsome feetlings'

Jumbotron fetish bombs thwack prosthetic lakes

Many walking, all stalked, petals flunked, muse creaks

Belly iron shines ruses on broke body stammering

Gleaming tribes of incestors mix humument milkshakes

Dissident riveted ruination suites salute frimpty wakes

Folded hands applaud above a budding

Jumbo pansy warping terminal aches

This indigenous earth fingers mensch pancakes

Ass ashy clutter trick everlasting too leaning

A ginger ancestor played human by takes

My jumbo warp fetish threadbare on the make

AFTER HARRYETTE MULLEN

I like to be entered

by worry on your

average day. And

smothered by a

confit of feelings

when the air is loosely

weighted, and gravy.

When the weather

is avid in insolence

I enjoy revisiting

an elegy while going

my masked and busy

way. I dig the activation

inside the singer's memory

of a single white rose

dropped from my sister's

hand onto a military

casket in which the

empty body of our

father lay. The whole

flash fills me with

resignation, which

doesn't interfere

with my little list

of tasks manifested

by will to feign

putting me under

practicality's sway. I

wrote it out on an

orange piece of paper

circulated to con people

into voting a particular

way. In the future our

votes will be pointed

to as futile attempts

to forestall a great

American fade? I'm

free to take little

pains. To swaddle

them effectually

and give everything

else such as I do

not own away.

FOR ED SANDERS
& KATE BERRIGAN

I FELT LIKE AN AMPUTATED LEG

He looked about as
inconspicuous as a
tarantula on a slice
of angel food. He
stood like a statue,
and after a long
time he smiled.
He had a battered
face that looked
like it had been
hit by everything
but the bucket of
a dragline. He spoke
almost dreamily, as
if he was all by him-
self, out in the woods,
picking johnny-jump-
ups. He looked like
a man who could
take a bank single-
handed—even in
those clothes. Just
folded, like a hand-
kerchief or a hinge.
The green stone in
his stickpin was not

quite as large as an
apple. It was him all
right, taken in a strong
light, and looking as
if he had no more
eyebrows than a
French roll. His blond
hair was arranged, by
art or nature, in three
precise ledges,
which reminded me
of steps, so that I
didn't like them.
He moved away
like a dancer, his
body almost motion-
less from the waist
up. His hair was
dark with blood,
the beautiful blond
ledges were tangled
with blood and
some thick grayish
ooze, like primeval
slime. There was
a trickle as black
as dirty oil at the
corner of his mouth.
In his coat loose
match folders, a
gold pencil clipped
to a pocket, & two
thin cambric

handkerchiefs as
fine and white
as powdered snow.
A face with bone
under the skin,
fine drawn like
a Cremona violin.
He wore a dark
red tie with black
spots on it and
the spots kept
dancing in front
of my eyes. That
a man occasion-
ally smoked a
stick of tea, a
man who looked
as if any touch
of the exotic
would appeal to
him. He was
silent a moment,
as if deciding
something. Give
him enough time
and pay him en-
ough money and
he'll cure anything
from a jaded hus-
band to a grasshop-
per plague. Men
would sneak in on
him too, big strong

guys that roared like
lions around their
offices and were
all cold mush under
their vests. They
probably sounded
like words. The
sound was like a
hen having hic-
cups. He was a
dark, good-looking
lad, with plenty
of shoulders and
shiny smooth
hair and the peak
on his rakish cap
made a soft sha-
dow over his eyes.
He had a cigar-
ette in the corner
of his mouth
and he held his
head tilted a little,
as if he liked to
keep the smoke
out of his nose.
It was the kind
of carelessness
that was meant
to be noticed. He
was so polite I
wanted to carry
him out of the

room to show
my appreciation.
He stood just
inside the corridor
door looking as
if he had been
cast in bronze.
He looked like
a bum. He wore
it about where
a house wears a
weather vane. He
had a big flat face
and a highbridged
fleshy nose that
looked as hard as
the prow of a cruiser.
If he had cleaned up
a little and dressed
in a white night-
gown, he would
have looked like a
very wicked Roman
senator. His skin
was as fresh as a
rose petal. His eye-
brows were coal
black, like the ceiling
and the floor. His
face was as fresh as
an angel's wing. "He
would photograph
like Isadora Duncan."

He was sitting with-
out a movement,
his eyes closed, his
head bent forward
a little, as if he had
been asleep for an
hour. Then he sat
like a stone lion
outside the Public
Library. He was
a windblown blossom
of some two hundred
pounds with freckled
teeth and the mellow
voice of a circus
barker. He stood in
front of me splay-
legged, holding my
open wallet in his
hand, making scrat-
ches on the leather,
with his right thumb-
nail, as if he just
liked to spoil things.
He looked like
a waiter in a
beachtown flytrap.
And I had seen
him with an Army
Colt looking like a
toy in his fist, stepping
softly through a broken
door. His smile

was as stiff as a fro-
zen fish. His long
fingers made move-
ments like dying but-
terflies. His words
were coming so fast
they were leapfrogging
themselves. He jerked
as if I had slapped
his face. His eyes were
going over my face
line by line, corpuscle
by corpuscle, like Sherlock
Holmes with his mag-
nifying glass or Thorn-
dyke with his pocket
lens. And after all
his psychic racket
is a temporary racket
for any one place.
He came back softly,
holding his pork
pie under his arm,
debonair as a French
count in a college
play. He was waiting
for something, a
sound like nothing
else on earth. He
had small, hungry,
heavy-lidded eyes,
as restless as fleas.
His face changed

so completely that
it was as if another
man sat in his chair.
His face still looked
like a stone face.
At the end he
thought and then
spoke slowly and
what he said had
wisps of fog cling-
ing to it, like the
beads on a mous-
tache. His yellow
eyes lighted as if
with a new flame.
His hat was pushed
back on his black
curly hair and his
nose sniffed, like
the nose of a hunt-
ing dog. He puffed
his cigarette awk-
wardly, as if it was
too small for his
fingers to hold
with comfort.

AFTER RAYMOND CHANDLER

HOLLOCENE

How are we doing

notationally speaking?

We are feeling conspicuous

No amount of crypto-hasho

forear/blackbear

fiddling will make us not

have to get up

& pee while high

in this death to explosions

bean scenery underlay

Writing Anselm imitations

in a fucking café. Space goes

here. Approximate length

of limit stops behind, distraught

at not having hand held

Original crumbs wiped

off original arm

FOR & AFTER ANSELM HOLLO

HERE, TAKE THESE HERBS

For consciousness the world is decor: sentences cast about
For bodies in the exuberant wobble factory Q-Bert believes
In me in the dark to pass out and check yourself out gliding
By storefront windows searching for a feeling no one's felt
In the last twelve seconds lathered with coeval nightmare
Rhetoric of sociable extinction bashful as a wraith eking out
A line of image extract to sprinkle on a plenty reeling mind
In charge up the stairs came a 1-2-3 inning obsessed with
Posture and it's always curved in the jury pool agape like
Flatbed torture simulations tooling around the Village
Routine shapes of feeling come down hard: a gavel calling
Culture to order but I'm a bad criminal juror because
I've been mugged twice no appropriate response required
I talked the first mugger down from beating my fourteen-year-
Old ass into the ground as he walked me home across town
His likes included fucking listening to music being with friends
And drugs when he left he gave me five I think our long walk
& talk would make me an excellent juror (show of nods)

FUCK THAT SHIT

No, *that* shit.

CREATIVE RESPONSE

Who wants to read
just to think of things
to get sort-of paid
to say? I took German
once, returned it
asked the teacher
to fail me mid-term
so I could stop coming
by class (I don't exactly
believe in solutions).
We're back in time.
"Next Level: Michael
Boley's Importance."
There's gonna be goth
bathroom readings.
There's two weeks
off before the annual
major event. There
sucks, and doesn't
feel relaxed enough
to make noises in
a glandular series
of toxicolor johns.
You know you don't
believe in agreement.
At the press conference

they all agreed they
were alone, like western
art, tacitly. Dumpster
art on 4th and 3rd keeps
changing without
improvement. As if
I know, being closer
to mountains, what
becomes of the broken
hearted sign painter.
It was pleasant to be
called a lodestar
today. Did she say
lodestone? Either
way it was like, it
wasn't like, I don't
believe so much in
likeness, but I did
feel closer to my
environment for a
little while. I'm glad
I didn't turn into air
sentimental a risk as
back there, that didn't
take, seams-wise. It's
easier to write than
read in the dark
daylight that, right
now, taunts us with
the casual certainty
of a letter of recom-
mendation: I am
writing on behalf

of these here urbane
pigeons whose semi-
gorgeous cooing I
believe would lend
sophistication, wisdom
and a matter-of-fact
tonal space pierced
by inevitability to
your questionably
administered set of
necessities. What
matter the twisted
condition of some
of their legs? They
unlike most of your
typical prospects
are drawn to the
few remaining crack-
pots in our mutual
neck of the woods
who retain the pride
to keep from dressing
up in the process
of undressing, which
every pigeon knows
is just another surface
built to curry favor
with the mind a pretty
boss projects. Like LeBron
against the Mavs in
the 2011 NBA finals, these
pigeons, on that score
have already checked

out. You need to
admit the company
of these birds. As such
I give them my highest
recommendation.
Sincerely, Anselm
Berrigan, author of
five books of poetry,
most recently Notes
from Irrelevance, a
book-length poem
published in 2011
by Wave Books.

COMPLEMENTARY NOTEBOKE

After breaking its spine we notice

More clouds dressed up as brains

Writhing past towers all adrip

In grey snowlight. The Skids

Remind us both of that Brueghel

We ought to know, but everyone

From a distance is going natural

Goth. Another Pernod for Mr

Archer, please. Neon doomsters

Swear everything registered will

Be good, if not especially just.

Eventually the climate overpowers

Inaugural sentiment, breaking

All comers into lists of pursed O's

Melting down over candy, rejecting

Unasked-for snapshots of our

Tackish purple-lit carousel rides

By the Seine's inviting trashbag

Green currents. The anti-concussion

Rules can't keep up with evolving

Bodies hurtling themselves across

Numbered chalk lines for us watchers

Without guaranteed contracts. No

One truly broke fears that, exactly.

COMPATIBILITY MODES

Courtesy, being
something to the
sidecar, entered
a fat baby/pure
love version of
walled-in reality
with a fragrant
purple skin tone
to highlight our
tedious desolation.
Yes, it was a split
pea rallying an ache
of routines, but
to notice past an
uncertain point
would be to take
on the most primal
of glib characteristics
& wave antique
scaffolding at
the latest festival
of triaged intensity.
It's not that I
forget I have a body
I just get locked
back into it with
such numbing

vaguely medieval
littering within
localized thought
balloons. I hope
to find I can imagine
an utterly alien
eros by listening
for possible methods
of extraterrestrial sex:

1. Mutually unrecognizable masturbation.
2. Unconscious rear-to-rear ascension.
3. Telepathic stimulation of pleasure centres;
     a possibly manipulative-to-criminal act; yet
     what constitutes a crime for an alien species
     may also be totally unknown.
4. Extended absence as sexual act.
5. Extended proximity in catatonic stasis as sexual act.
6. Group Suspension.
7. Unknown.
8. As Like.
9. Unknowner.
10. Envelopment (total, as in bio-organic costume).
11. Sex acts as practical actions performed regularly
     even hourly in public, discreetly.
12. Cataclysmic eruption between ocean-sized entities.
13. Sex as minute distinction so as to be nearly
imperceptible.

forbearance at such
and such intervals
dating their markets
for purposes of
the deep flip out
I'm sure my mem
ories don't dissipate
fast enough. Coaster
children for sample
sale agree, if
embittered by the

CHASES DIRT

When faking feeling too ill to be
in school, and there's no phone
at home, the principals have to call
George. Major storm swelling out of the
rockies, into and out of this torso to
Plunder the Sun, a 3-in-1 credit rapport
with Score Power. And I, just sitting
here, am, don't try, cleansing Color
Products, for the prism that ere to Thor
commandeers our gas. Rental jagtron.
"All dem leettle pressures make you give
yourself too many corrosive gifts!" It is
not hard to be exhausted. Addington
—or any other thoughtless, when the
pressure's on, fuck—read the space
to add room to a weakness, a perfectly
obvious blind spot in the national
psyche, with advice. A poor-heeled gig
without the poor. Touch the color &
G belts my arm, but not so it hurts
physically. And anyone with the guts
to turn, their fine legs coming out of
the captain's head, off and thinking,
make fifty or a hundred thoughts about
it, is gonna get that torturing's a weakness.
Made the mistake of wanting to see if
the paint felt as vivid as it looked, twice.
Smack! Not toy. Cut to light when
boredom's certainty friezes; imagine
along the way who's doing it on vases.

FOR GEORGE SCHNEEMAN

BUBBLE METROPOLIS

misorder's closed captioning sponsored by 1-800-Got-Junk, visceral & lost brain

matter, on view, manchild's ultimate excursion to Drexciya, flocking faster

your adjunct carrier pigeon takes back the fritz, ashier than

the merkins of juvenile cowboys, prayers for alum in Lynch's mouth:

fools do as doom requests, on ashier blinkways, synchronizing beep-

leaves trail derogatory grease, mother bordering control, echo shirking coyote beep

faux flat necking skeletons ignore no standing here

misplaced attentiveness, booty alert, Compton's slapstick Jesus comes

the backplane entirely pink & unreal, refjorders the

surfboard fetish cakewalk, a zigzag, a minor gag,

leaning out of corners, flying canoes vanish into oceanic order

WITH LATASHA DIGGS

ASHEVILLE

hiding to let it work a sense of hoping to lose it to refuse its performance its conditions
and explanations tattled in rainbow loom doom strolling by the fan cave cue red receptacle
for used blood endowed in prodigal sucker perpetuity modern bleak redemption opening
the cinema for dumpy-souled laugh orientation at which (tires squealing) you could play citizen
scum scoring a reset hallway heretofore loading adjacent polar vortex muffling bears inducing
a transaction counter an incessant speed of affection to upgrade the trag-affect it was all splices
of enormity dunk-blocking the precog's morbidity incursion duking it out with scrolls and skrulls

high places in friends & the speed of promised growth in a version of
the present architecture dog shit meets used cracker at the site of eros
the local branch a person changing its name from sovereign to salamander
I give the guys with bad backs loose change they renew the visual sense you
know the weather's so lovely the rats can't say no we found their treaty with
the squirrels under a fake rock compromise in Tompkins Square high yield
checking to beat off rent bombing the fuck out of fuck its adopted son clarity's

what you say you think it's the emotion of cutdown day
getting in the conversation ray's mock-up of unilateral
securitay's breeding sites groping for intimacy between
poisons a sweetness picture picking off points for measure
preseason heroes know it's a feel-space legacy the decision
to decide when to make a prior show of showing prop up
the present with an ugly hand according to a composite mouth

& having invented your own logic
                    you can't use
                    walking with you

                                        elevate your friends into strangers

a moral suspicion
            in every layer
     of evolved definition

abstract concept overload

                                                    again is always something

                        I respond to arrangements

to replace my blank spaces

you remind me often
     of a desperation   to make brief

            those blank spaces

            someone adds an extra silence I felt-tipped it down the crosshatch
            went infinity flow my tears the policeman's neon blue fingers still probing its sass
            I do not remember technology I do not remember my father's entire body
            in exact detail I do not remember most of my education but all of the feeling
            all the endlessly fucking slow layering of every minute micro-jolt accreting there's
            not much about money to tell you don't already contain in your bulby knowledge
            shell the boundaries of boredom I found myself nodding against a grain

pangs of reality inside another fully beautified escape from daily to daily
particulars shit on canvas (see Brueghel at the movies) an addiction on discount
how that goblet get from there to there curl of a demon scream for raspberries
slumming with the counter-reformation among rainbow plastic sippy cup palettes
walking with a confident paranoia on retractable leash here hold my annihilus
the projection of luck onto others a ghastly utopia so says a bold divergence nudge
an American reveal a cop decked out in complaint to avoid this fate we must

strike against sleep
voxily benumbed
connect yr charger

it in fact is hard to touch you
true, our history a series of
assignations the utility of personal
difficulty & its attendant logics
breaking up into mutual doses
of rejection. No more poetics

a binge of opening acts splits apart into Orders of Experience:

what are your reigning rules for yourself mr hard playa on the less than average
arbitrary temporal marker of the over-processed moment? Grainy drowning bat
in underground lunchbox? Paranoid crab pincing toe chubs from eternity's
couch-thing? Seaweed dumps under layers of biodegradable friendship collections?
That magisterial pounding just out in front of your skull to the right is your source
of tangential authority, ready to self-skewer your dingity when politics require you

to pull the old blankie out from under your feet? Your electronic self-image array
remind you of the knowing dirtbag teachers who've never understood one fucking
thing you've said? They're still better than the baiters of bears waving structure
at you disguised as wit and fortune, no? You're forty-one. You dunked your children
in the grease holding them by their faces. Everything charging up from behind
is unhinged and consoling. Fortunately for the times you despise explanation

partial azure balloon stomp doggie popped out back

you put these tiny flower bugs in your pocket?

the distance between

those two positions

is a little immeasurable

but I miss the absence of the person

who filled the absence of

another person—I miss

the second person

& that missing sucks to say

here we all are leaving

"to be"

here

a year later I'm where

the light is right

to prepare for introduction

as a fixed act

which renders demotive

me a non-unified

significance ahead

of sanctioned leeching

wrap the box set book addiction in transparent dragon skin after hiding
the seahorsies' eyelashes in a too-big stroller's expectant demi-grime thank you
for the nod out in collaboration with medical relocation I'm always a touch late
to ten baroque minutes away from a bad repair job in gravel kittywalks where
unnameable fluidity unlimited only by the flow of your distressed clarity of material

curated in absentia
by a fondness for absentia

we must liberate the still
from their tempos and stories

for a bio the ghost wrote an
approximate likeness of a voice

a blocked punt could paste a face
onto so many books to stand and read

in aisles and not quite pay for stewarding
homelike a fella in his mutterings can't

believe they don't drop bombs & grenades
on this place & he's a follower & I avoid him

by standing right in front of him my fears are local
the big guy's muttering stink shaped up once in a while

is no headlock inducer I'm worried about boys who
can hurt me and not being any good at anything

so reality turns out to be a little more
convoluted than its agencies

the desk form virgiling itself in a video bank for macro-minor instance we get to disbelieve in surfacing

lording critique over death

let's shuffle our personalized logistics:
at home exhausted warmth on the street
business ephemeral concrete mollified innerware

I do not have persona stamina

micro-cottage industries of we

bleeding out from waves

my hand is alive says a phone

near the intersection of 9th

& Charlie Parker Place a hell-

sun limps via intervention

into dragon-form pre-pickup

auto-perspiration downwind

from dog-run alone between

steps with my man-thoughts

my klutzy wager thunks too

much white in the sky-motion

pleather heaven falcon scores I missed a walk-off wild pitch struck aquarium

with laconic emphasis a turning point witnessed avoiding masses in my habits

accreting metal staring up at shoe gazers & searching for Udhrī poets greeted by perfect realspeak on no-fault divorce I know the wrong eight hundred years ago

its default user a forward collision warning sigh to shake down whitey apocalypse

twins rapture mutants to Jupiter the eternal executioner choppable by Norse axe

confused about what to cop piling down first half stats wrong's extra-secret wrong

but your spliced idea of life demands turns hunting down a drunk pill to split

<1.5>new year's resolution go full-blown cheeseball tweak tenement rooftop wind supplies

readymade answers all nonthinking elegies emptied in ignorant lists sliming the otherwise

bottomless beading secret lover of pigeons throw glasses I mean skyscraping needles

phlebotomizing the uptown skyframe I myself heck in a cuff the plain dysfunction

of inevitable decay-reversal turning ploy a stance on potential self-approximation refused entry

to that shipwreck in liftoff if you're trained as I can't be to steer vehicles one compromise elides

another one death-stick weakens selection (panel yet to be colored) why not be exuberant typed

the career diplomat like stealth has been an inspiration (raw materials: hot rationales in astroturf shirts)

all I ever wanted will be ceaseless vibrations warding off resentiment behind the plain layers in view

finishing studies insert flyleaf
   the shumpert jersey marches off
      to intermission the platitude dome
         an arming of character into arenalight
         I'm a reel-to I know this propping
            digital light & she will have her tree
               just behind her name carved onto a
                  passable rectangle solidity feints

wearability are there any donuts
to shake into view from the art shop
on this sublet of a mantle? I say &
everything wrong in slight enigma
launch parsing sensation to loosen
shivers from a coming bundle of ofs
wrapped by gift certification: 30 at
grassroots, 10 at st. mark's theater
25 cents for bengal stripes on
a bottle cap's inner lid one brings
a processed mistake to temporary
home & unleashes elegiac sentiment
(the art is in the arrangement)

AN ALPHABET FOR NOBODY

A is for Atalantavan

B is for Broke-Ass Daddy

C is for Carmelo Back On D

D is for Deer Antler Spray

E is for Pink Eye

F is for Fainting Lines In Sky

G is for Grace Lake

H is for Here Comes A Regular

I is for I Don't Get It

J is for Jackoff Algorhythm

K is for Kenward

L is for Lamination Sweets

M is for Meatwind

N is for Can Of Nap

O is for Ionized Air

P is for Pick Up The House

Q is for Quackpot

R is for Roto-Dendrum-Tisserie-Virus-Rooter

S is for Sandwich Eats Face

T is for Boneless Or Traditional

U is for Fetishized Negation

V

W is for Work Emails We Have Known

Y is for Whatever

Z is for Moustache

POST-CRYPT

& WHAT DOES "NEED" MEAN?

FOR THE PARISH HALL
AT ST. MARK'S CHURCH

Having written the some or none
questions to be addressed, ignored
and otherwise dissolved behind
us as prelude, I have to note
I should have said something
other than East Village, which is
a real estate term designed to—
& it did so successfully—
subdivide the lower east side
& greenwich village simultaneously
back, oh, about 30-plus years
ago & maybe it's not inaccurate
to place the "what's it mean" question
in a real estate context but the
term, east village, feels shittier &
shittier to me by the day & down-
town is another play on dislocation
anyway—do you feel as if form has
collapsed? If so, you can't be a
pigeon, alas, as I imagine
for pigeons downtown *is* sign
sigh, thing, active nothing
& something else all at once—I
can imagine, can't I? Adaptably?
Post-pragmatically? Wondering what
realism means to me? I don't think

the Church roof leaks as much
as it used to/I can't remember
if the clock tower's ever really
known what time it is since that
lightning bolt struck it some 17 yrs
ago/it's possible Lamantia is still
reading somewhere on this very spot
with anyone out here, or is it in
there, listening at all? You do still
get to say, even the day after
election day, peace, if so, no? The
question of what need means gets
bound up with what care means
& that's no way to do this. I
wondered for a long time & still
do inside & around my privacy
at times, whatever that isn't, & it
—highly overused and floating that it—
mostly isn't. Most of what I do is
listen. Most of the time I've spent
in this space I've spent listening:
listening to poets, hundreds of
them, dancers, prose writers,
painters, comedians, eulogizers,
hearfelt jackoff poseurs, cab drivers
black-angel-wing-wearing anti-Giuliani
ranters in half/Japanese half/English,
gossipers at breaks, accusers, hecklers
Jimmy the sextant's constant whistling
by day, anxious amused murmurers
among the among-the-fews who
accumulate into so many you
wonder how so much listening

gets done by so many micro-slants
on the wing. Back up, back to need
what that may be, because I've
listened long enough to know
I *need* to be doing it, to practice
listening, to get better at it and
get at getting it better in the fucked
up constellation that is your head
becoming poetry, & to be encouraged
by the mess & the many responses
of which hate, or let's say, today
anger, fear, disconsolation, is just
one of many. Why be afraid of hate?
It is only there, I keep listening to
a man I never knew say. I want
lately to find out why in poems
space is not an illusion, why when
it's working you're put right there
immediately, unconditionally, and
then you have to move, however
bewildered, or maybe because you
are, because I know in the sudden
sharp jab of recognition (& what
I think when I think about sex—
it ain't necessarily death) I mean
I know it quite precisely parallel
to doing it, that it only gets to be
happening *when* I'm listening
& I go to places where listening
is actually the point—and there
aren't many places, there aren't
that many that want more than
the show of listening, that don't

let language get so disconnected
from reality all you're stuck with
is definition as another emblem
of fear—I keep going and coming
back to this place for that & by
the way, you do get, right, how
truly fucking strange, if ordinary
it is, to be breathing, here, doing
this with a voice? But one might
need to do that, have it be given
that one can do all that & without
conventions: the old ones, the
currents, the ones placed in your
head by you or anyone else, the
theoretical, philosophical, political
behavioral conventions dressed
up in the costume of underpinning
the being-in-a-group con, the lonely
awful conventions of anonymity
(you ever wonder if your muse isn't
a landlord?) Everything I'm pulling
from the register is a question – – – –
I come here to listen without…
without convention, to listen
against, to listen for convention's
lack, to hear it, the art, its off-
shoots, foils, companions &
highly troubled organs disappear
by doing, being in that—it's easy
to do & gets harder as the shapes
get shapelier. You really think
language failed? How come it's
language, not words? Because

words aren't language?
Because maybe you cede so
much of what possibility is
to bubbles of discernment?
to representation? to instant
understanding? I think I need to
not know in order to listen (to
begin/ it all pours in then)/ I need
things that don't go together
to be put in time together. & I
do need that out front. I re-
member sitting in this room in
1987, not quite fifteen, sobbing
uncontrollably at my half-sister
Kate's memorial—she'd been
hit and killed by a motorcycle
not a week earlier on Houston
St coming over to take my brother
and me to a movie. I remember
wondering if I should get up
and say something—inside
all that crying what I felt was
the impulse to put some
words in the air. Then it was
as if I didn't speak for another
year, & that's a feeling, not
another fucking metaphor. Is
there any metric for how much
pain this room has absorbed
& had reconverted into music?
Into humor? Among other wild
kindnesses. Penniless Politics
always said music as shorthand

for prosody. You'd be right to
paint the word unobjective on
my face. I have often sometimes
wished there was something like
the reading channel & I could
turn that on and listen without
transporting via feets my personally
bent frame to the reading itself,
since I'm weirdly bad at listening
to recordings of poems, maybe
because I'm not present to let
my nerves—that's right, I'm
nervous when other people read
their shit—get defeated by what
actually fucking happens, even
if it's the lamest thing in the world
though sometimes lame is better
than boring & I'm not sorry to say
boredom is a bit of a professional
value, plus that whole fail better
thing, you feel good about that
right now, & you know, it's kind
of cowardly to just stop, and, oh
duchamp, make an industry out
of supposedly stopping to swallow
as fact, what, you think I could be
especially coherent today? What'd
the self-composed monster maker
say? The world today doesn't make
sense so why should I paint pictures
that do. Where was I? Busy being
told to decompose. I know I got
ten minutes but this sketchbook

which I bought for eight bucks
today, the day before the time
I get to say today and have it both
be and mean a now-machine has
kind of short pages, which is a
problem I'm counting on—Ted
Greenwald was the one who said
the Project's about putting the
work out front, & if you want an
ecstatic and devastated or joyful
and perennially disturbed distressed
life—well, we get that anyway—I'm
hearing that sense of, it has to
be, the shit has to be, the mind,
of such nameless depths that
being serious's just one of many
ordinary facts of commitment
& not some dolled-up badge
of complexity. That's a tricky
difficult, old, inherited useless,
changed, rearranged, by me, no:
when did change just become
rearrangement? Which is really
richer, riskier? You leaning on
implied or unemployed meaning?
The web's old enough to be another
version of aged thing. If I wanted
everything so flat I'd have done
better in my life by way of hopeless
addiction. I come to things
here because this place has
been imperfectly available
to care & care for. That's always run

through an interconnection
of mouths, that care. Dangerous
reflex. You wonder who's going
to challenge you to adapt. You
wonder if the adaptation proposed,
if so, ain't as slow as your own
evolution. Are we supposed to
turn into birds? Again? Lives
go where there's no forms. That
leaves us where to go? Another
kind of pain, the living question.
Here, like anywhere that's fought
however knowingly & unknowingly
for the right to be itself, on its own
terms, which only means letting
the folks who care enough to really
come through figure out how to
do that too, without much
interference, here has to be able to
freak out on itself out of loyalty
to itself, itself not being made
of any singular thingitation.
Here's another kind of question:
my mom, being a poet who lived
in this city & this particular
neighborhood for parts of the
'60s, '70s, '80s, and '90s, who still
visits a few times a year, who
said she wrote things to be
read and listened to specifically
in this room, and who shared
a birthday yesterday with the
anxious horror of our planet-wreck

of an election, once said to me on
the phone, "I can't find out what
the streets of New York look like
by reading anyone's poems any-
more." She didn't mean what
they seem like, feel like, but
what they look like. You ever
try to describe a whole street?
I assumed I had to try, and
wound up sitting down on
one of the benches out here
on the corner of 10th and 2nd
and wrote the following,
which is no consolation, but
was never meant to be:

WHAT THE STREETS
LOOK LIKE

Mom: the sweet rotted
summer stench still
taps the nasal cavity
inside breezes several
times per block. I have
a greater empathy for
pigeons after two months
at work in the unnatural
country, & find it
instinctively nerve-
wracking to remove my
wallet from its pocket
here in town despite

the general lack of threat.
The streets look grey,
nonplussed, post-
pubescent relative to
ancient times but
nonetheless grid-wizened
in the face of an ever-
changing lineup of
banks, bars, and specialty
shops with their weak
signs and distant tones
("lighting"). Second Ave
is giving up, slowly
its cheap depth store-
front by storefront.
One feels less than
nostalgic for the like-
lihood of being mugged
but likelihood itself
feels less than evident
unless one is unstable
and unspoken coming
to dreaming pushing
a stroller over variously
cracked slabs of concrete
each block yet greets the
wheels with. The right
part of the y heading
west on tenth between
2nd and 3rd is still tree-
lined and aristocratic
as feint, though its
sidewalk looks like

late Auden's smoked
cheeks. I loathe it,
amiably, when Sylvie
is asleep.

I can't end this with that.
I don't want to end with
loathing. So I'll read this
poem by my stepfather
Douglas Oliver, who lived
here in nyc in the late '8os
and early '90s, when death
seemed everywhere, & to
walk down the street, our
street, was to daily take on
a gauntlet of harassment
and possible violence, &
the politics so often felt
hopeless. This, written
here, I believe, is called

FOR KIND

Kindness acts idly or unnaturally,
leads you into fear. Act in kind.
Kindness makes you idle, worse, unnatural.
Don't be afraid of the darkness of kind;
for it's the birth darkness, vertical twist
of opening lips in the night: life that follows
belongs to you in kind. Don't be frightened
of darkness of origin: it is this darkness,

similar tints of our flesh in the night
of kind. The kind you are, with slim
mammalian chest, and, walking to the bathroom,
hip-swag: how naturally your walk sways
in kind. You are humankind,
my kind, kind to me, born well and gentle.
We believe in kind:
birth, origin, descent, nature,
sex, upbringing, race, our natural property,
so many things we naturally have
and have no need to struggle for
merely out of kindness to each other, or,
worse, to struggle for unnaturally

11/09/16

Note: this poem was written to be read at The Poetry Project's "(Re)Defining Downtown" event, was typed and finished under the influence of the election results on 11/08/16, and was a response to the following set of loose questions: "What's it mean for The Poetry Project to be The Poetry Project right now, in the East Village, in 2016, which is or was considered 'downtown' at points? Is 'downtown' a sign, a sigh, a thing, an active nothing, or a something else? Can we have a retrospective season and dissolve nostalgia at the same time? Is there anyone out there listening at all? (If so, peace). Do poets in this town still need real physical centers to go experience the work out front? And what does 'need' mean? And what does 'real physical centers' mean? And what does 'out front' mean?"

NOTES & ACKS

Versions of some of these poems have appeared in the following print and electronic publications: *Avantlache*, *BathHouse Journal* (bhjournal.net), *The Café Review*, *Court Green*, *Elective Affinities* "cooperative anthology of contemporary u.s. poetry" (electiveaffinitiesusa.blogspot.com), Hyperallergic.com, *Lemon Hound* (lemon-hound.com), *Past Simple* (pastsimple.org), Poets.org, *The Recluse*, *Test Centre*, *Theme Can* (theme-can.com), *Vertaallab 8* (ooteoote.nl), *The Volta* (thevolta.org) & *Washington Square Review*.

Some poems herein also appeared in the following chapbooks: *Anna's Half/Anselm's Half*, a dos-à-dos work with Anna Moschovakis published by NewLights Press; *Skasers*, published by Flowers & Cream, with John Coletti, who wrote my poems, and vice versa; & *Sure Shot* published by the good folks from Overpass Books.

"Self-Portrait with Lasers," "veins & modes & veins & modes . . .," "Loading," "Loadeding," "Inward Branding Mechanism 2: Lonesome Sabotage," "Inward Branding Mechanism" & "An Alphabet for Nobody" first appeared in *Loading*, a collaborative book with visual artist Jonathan Allen, published by Brooklyn Arts Press.

"Compatibility Modes" was written at the request of Suzie Silver who, along with Christopher Kardambikis & Jasdeep Khaira, edited/curated the video/print anthology *Strange Attractors: Investigations in Non-Humanoid Extraterrestrial Sexualities*.

"Bubble Metropolis" is a collaboration with LaTasha N. Nevada Diggs, and was commissioned by the Center for Book Arts in New York City.

"Illanelle" was written as part of a somewhat indescribable nine-poet collaborative endeavor organized by Buzz Evers several years ago, and while most of the work from that weekend remains in a mysterious form of stasis, this one poem I wrote—when requested to write a villanelle borrowing some language from somewhere, so I used a few things from Harryette Mullen's book-length poem *Muse & Drudge*, which, along with Kevin Davies's poem "Karnal Bunt," rewrote my head significantly in the late 1990s—managed to escape stasis because I kept it, because I liked it.

"I Felt Like An Amputated Leg" owes itself to Raymond Chandler's novel *Farewell, My Lovely*.

"Seven" was written right before walking into a classroom of second-graders to talk with them about poetry. "the green lake is awake" was later written with two of those second-graders.

"17 Mini-Essays on *The Collected Writings of Joe Brainard*" was written for BOMB magazine upon their request for a creative response to *The Collected Writings of Joe Brainard*, who wrote many mini-essays. The titles are mine. The lines are from various works of JB's.

"Asheville" takes its title and rough method of composition (interlace sketches then transfer the composite layout to a support) from the 1948 painting *Asheville* by Willem de Kooning.

My grateful thanks to the many editors, publishers, collaborators, and influencers, known and unknown, who helped make these things happen. They were never meant to all go together until they did. [more thanks and dedications t/k] —AB